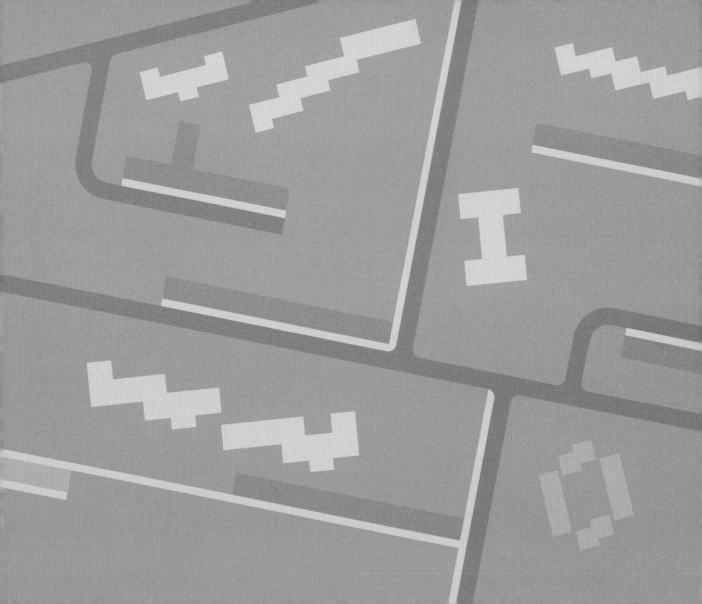

Modernist Council Housing 1946–1981
London Estates

MODERNIST COUNCIL HOUSING   1946–1981

London Estates

Thaddeus Zupančič

FUEL

For Elain Harwood

CONTENTS

A Better Tomorrow

Thaddeus Zupančič

Between 1945 and 1949, the London County Council (LCC), the largest and most ambitious English municipal authority of its day, built 44,000 new homes within its boundaries.[1] It was necessary to build quickly and expediently: the Luftwaffe had inflicted a heavy toll on the capital, killing 19,415 people and damaging 709,528 buildings, of which 52,267 were demolished and 17,171 beyond repair.[2] The LCC, which at that time comprised 28 metropolitan borough councils, alongside the City of London, embarked on a rebuilding and redevelopment programme like no other. There is no district of London, other than aristocratic Belgravia and Mayfair, that does not have council estates of significant size.[3]

The *County of London Plan* (1943) by Patrick Abercrombie and J.H. Forshaw, Architect to the LCC, was adopted as a model, proposing a 'conditioned yet comprehensive redevelopment' of the capital.[4] Despite post-war austerity, relatively generous funding was available for housing, since the incoming Labour government allowed local authorities to borrow at low rates from the Public Works Loans Board.[5] The government however, retained control of the councils' housing programmes which had to be approved by the Ministry of Health and Housing (until 1951) or the Ministry of Local Government and Planning (thereafter). Consequently, requested loans might be rejected or subjected to modification. In 1949 the government also published *The Housing Manual*, which established standards in the design, planning, layout and construction of all public housing, to which post-war local authorities had to conform.[6] Equally influential was a 1961 special committee report into housing space values, which recommended

larger, centrally heated homes,[7] proposing, for instance, that 70 square metres should be the minimum for a four-person flat.[8] Between 1969 and 1980 observance of these 'Parker Morris Standards', named after chairman of the committee, was mandatory in public housing.

In July 1945, LCC housing became the responsibility of the newly formed Department of Housing and Valuation,[9] a confirmation that speed and economy had taken almost total precedence over design. The first post-war schemes by borough councils were similarly as dour, prompting Walter Segal, the future guru of self-building in Lewisham, to point out that a slower pace would allow more opportunity for reflection and selection.[10]

However, there were two exceptions to this rule. The first was Finsbury in north London and its council's ongoing work with Tecton, the celebrated modernist practice established by Berthold Lubetkin. After finishing the Finsbury Health Centre (1935–8), Tecton was commissioned to design two housing projects, but both were postponed until after the war. The more famous Spa Green Estate, comprising three blocks with elaborately patterned exteriors, was completed by the executive architects Skinner & Lubetkin after the dissolution of Tecton in 1947. The second exception was the City of Westminster's competition for a 12-hectare (30-acre) housing site in Pimlico, won by Philip Powell and Hidalgo Moya in 1946. The competition brief, Powell recalled, 'encouraged adventure, as well as more pious virtues of caution'.[11] The resulting Churchill Gardens Estate was constructed over 15 years from 1948, with the first phase completed in summer of 1951. Eventually housing nearly

6,000 people, it is a much-loved, unapologetically modernist housing scheme. It was also the only major project in Abercrombie's *County of London Plan* to be completed.[12]

Simultaneously, a campaign waged by architects and the architectural press against the poor design of LCC estates, led to a December 1949 report that recommended responsibility for housing be returned to the Architect's Department. The LCC's Architect to the Council, Robert Matthew, created a new Housing Division under John Whitfield Lewis with around 250 architects and assistants working in small groups. Outsiders given senior posts included Philip Powell's brother Michael and Colin Lucas, formerly of Connell, Ward & Lucas. It was Lucas's formidable reputation that protected the younger staff as they developed the most radical schemes.[13] Together with its three other divisions (Schools, Planning and General Works), the LCC Architect's Department soon became the foremost architectural practice in the world.[14] Robert Matthew retained his role until 1953 when he was succeeded by Leslie Martin (1953–6). Martin's successor was Hubert Bennett (1956–71), who was Architect to both the LCC and the Greater London Council (GLC), which replaced the LCC in 1965. He was followed by Roger Walters (1971–8), F.B. Pooley (1978–80) and P.E. Jones (until 1986, when the GLC was abolished). In the Housing Division, Whitfield Lewis was succeeded by K.J. Campbell (1959–74) and G.H. Wigglesworth (1974–80).

The first large housing scheme by the reinvigorated LCC Architect's Department was the strikingly modernist Ackroydon Estate (1953) in Wimbledon, which was promptly declared 'a triumph' in the architectural press.[15] Another group in the Housing Division worked on an efficient plan for maisonettes, which were incorporated into an 11-storey slab block with gallery access.[16] First built at the Gascoyne Estate (1952–4) in Homerton, these slabs were clearly modelled on Le Corbusier's Unité d'Habitation building in Marseille (1947–52), which was much admired by LCC architects and almost mandatory to visit. John Partridge recalled: 'Stan Amis and I duly made this pilgrimage (in a pre-war Morris with leaking petrol tank stopped with chewing gum), returning in total awe of the great master.'[17] The LCC subsequently dotted various iterations of them all over London, most famously at the Alton West Estate in Roehampton, a scheme on which Partridge and Amis worked. Slabs became an integral part of the low- and high-rise mixed developments that formed the dominant housing ideology of the 1950s.[18] There were, however, problems with their mass, which created issues with overshadowing and inflexibility of orientation.[19] Far greater potential was offered by the 'point block', a high-rise block with the circulation and services in the central core.

The earliest LCC high-rise point block was Oatlands Court, built in Southfields, in 1953. Designed by Colin Lucas, it was greatly admired by the architectural historian Ian Nairn: 'Compact, not too tall (eleven storeys), with one of those plans, immediately lucid, which architects dream of, fuss over, but rarely achieve.'[20] A little later, similar blocks were built on the nearby Ackroydon Estate.

The large Alton Estate was divided between two teams of LCC architects. The first, led by Rosemary Stjernstedt, designed the Alton East section (1952–5), inspired by Scandinavian modernism and Swedish high-rise *punkthus* (translated as 'point block', the origin of the term). The second, led by Colin Lucas, designed Alton West (1952–61). They adhered rigorously to an expressive Corbusian brutalism, applied across a range of forms including slabs, points, low-rise maisonette blocks and housing for older people.

An interesting synthesis were the 16-storey blocks combining maisonettes and flats, first designed by Edward Hollamby for the Silwood Estate in Rotherhithe (1958–62).[21] Somewhat taller were the blocks of cross-over, 'scissor' type maisonettes on the Pepys Estate in Deptford (1963–73). These had initially been tested at the Lincoln Estate in Poplar

(1960–62),[22] but later discontinued due to the high cost of their complex construction.[23]

Until 1965, only five of the metropolitan boroughs had borough architects.[24] Other councils relied on their own engineers and surveyors, as well as employing architects working in private practice, known as consulting architects. The best examples of work by consulting architects during the 1950s were the Golden Lane Estate by Chamberlin, Powell & Bon for the City of London, and projects by a panel of architects for Bethnal Green.

In 1951, the City organised an open competition for the Golden Lane Estate, the first major architectural competition in England since that for Churchill Gardens. The new estate from the outset attracted young professionals, including one architect, doctors, clergymen and married students.[25] Today it comprises a 17-storey block of flats, three low-rise blocks of flats, five blocks of maisonettes plus a community centre, swimming pool and tennis court.

Also in 1951, the nearby Bethnal Green council appointed a panel of architects to help them with their housing programme: Donald Hamilton, Wakeford & Partners; Skinner, Bailey & Lubetkin; Powell & Moya; Yorke, Rosenberg and Mardall; and Fry, Drew, Drake and Lasdun.[26] With the exception of Powell & Moya, they all went on to design housing schemes for the borough. The best are Lubetkin's swansong – the elegant and greatly admired Cranbrook Estate; and Denys Lasdun's extraordinary cluster blocks – with subsidiary residential towers linked to a core containing stairs and lifts, they were developed to suit the irregular and restricted slum clearance and redevelopment sites.[27]

Other prominent metropolitan borough consulting architects included Frederick Gibberd (Hackney); Howes & Jackman (Tottenham, Stoke Newington), George, Trew & Dunn (Battersea); Clifford Culpin & Partners (Wandsworth); and Co-operative Planning (Southwark, Hackney and Poplar). Construction companies (most notably Wates, which had its own architectural department run by Kenneth W. Bland), also contributed to schemes for local councils (Lambeth, Redbridge), as well as continuing with their own projects.

The reorganisation of London's local government in 1965 saw the creation of the GLC. Covering a much greater area than the LCC, its 32 new London borough councils (plus the City of London) assumed larger responsibilities for housing and planning. Accordingly, the London Government Act 1963 introduced the statutory post of architect for each of the boroughs and, 'as the case may be', for the City.[28]

The most celebrated of these was Sydney Cook at the new borough of Camden. Cook, formerly borough architect at Holborn, recruited some of the best young talent, one of the finest being Neave Brown,[29] who designed two of the most remarkable post-1965 council estates in London: the Dunboyne Road Estate (1971–7) in Gospel Oak and Rowley Way, part of the Alexandra & Ainsworth Estate (1972–9).

Westminster balanced the work of its new Department of Architecture and Planning with competitions: that for the rebuilding of Lillington Street (held already in 1961 and assessed by Philip Powell), was won by John Darbourne who formed a partnership with Geoffrey Darke to develop the scheme. The initial phase of their Lillington Gardens Estate was constructed in 1964–8 and became the first low-rise, high-density council estate in the capital. It earned numerous accolades, starting with the 1969 Award for Good Design in Housing, an honour sponsored by the Secretary of State for the Environment in collaboration with the Royal Institute of British Architects (RIBA).

During the period 1968–1980, the borough of Islington won the most Awards for Good Design in Housing.[30] Their Architecture Department, directed by Alf Head, complemented its own projects (Spring Gardens in Highbury, for example) with commissions from private practices. The very first post-1965 Islington Housing Development Area, Canonbury (Stage 1) Section 1 (Marquess Road), was designed by Darbourne & Darke and built between 1966–76;[31] the final project for the borough by the same practice, Seaforth Crescent in Highbury (1979–80), was hailed as 'something special' in the *Architects' Journal*.[32]

Borough architects in south London were just as active, particularly F.O. Hayes at Southwark (previously borough architect at Camberwell) and Edward Hollamby at Lambeth. Southwark's largest project was the Aylesbury Estate (1967–76, currently being demolished), but the most dramatic was Kate Macintosh's stunning Dawson's Heights Estate (1966–72) in Dulwich, which she called a 'Chinese puzzle of differing types, to be assembled in various combinations.'[33]

Edward Hollamby's vision for Lambeth was simple: 'We all accept that we are not just dealing with housing as such. We are building a community.'[34] One of his earliest appointments was George Finch, who had already made his name at the LCC. In the case of Finch's eight almost identical 22-storey towers with 80 maisonettes each – the first of which was Holland Rise House in Stockwell (1966–7) – the impression that each maisonette resembles a little house is more apparent here than in any other block of the period.[35] His Lambeth Towers (completed 1971) is a sinuous brutalist building constructed on a near-impossible 0.2-hectare (half-acre) site.

By that time, high-rises were – almost – on their way out, at least for the time being. Between 1956 and 1967 the government offered subsidies for the building of high-rise flats that increased with the height of the tower.[36] In 1968, the partial collapse of Ronan Point in Newham killed four people, turning public opinion firmly against high-rises – as well as against the system of 'industrialised' building, which had allowed for speedy construction. The problem with the latter was its peculiarly British application in the 1960s. Driven by profit and inadequately supervised, too often the results were botched and slapdash.[37]

Despite this, housing programmes remained a source of immense municipal pride: in 1971 Croydon Council reported that there were 19,100 'council units of accommodation' in the borough.[38] The GLC had similarly been active, building 26,000 new dwellings between 1965 and 1969.[39]

The last great hurrah of the GLC and its Department of Architecture and Civic Design, the successor to the LCC Architect's Department, was Thamesmead: 'basically a working-class Barbican, and if it were in EC1 rather in SE28 the price of a flat would be astronomical'.[40] Its architecturally most intriguing structures – the linear blocks of Coralline Walk and Binsey Walk – are now demolished.

Both the GLC and London boroughs continued to commission work from private practices, the GLC most famously from Ernő Goldfinger (who designed the Balfron Tower as part of the Brownfield Estate in Poplar, and the Cheltenham Estate, with Trellick Tower, in North Kensington), and Alison and Peter Smithson (architects of the now partially demolished Robin Hood Gardens).

The effect of Margaret Thatcher's Housing Act 1980 – 'to give security of tenure, and the right to buy their homes, to tenants of local authorities and other bodies'[41] – was seismic. By 1989 only 12 percent of the population gave council housing as their preferred form of tenure, compared to 20 percent in 1966.[42]

The Right to Buy was the largest privatisation in the country and proved extremely popular. The promotion of reduced state intervention – Thatcher called it 'throwing back the frontiers of state' – was a stark contrast to the position of Conservative party leaders 30 years earlier: that housing was 'the first of the social services'. At that time their target remained 300,000 new houses a year and they emphasised: 'There should be no reduction of houses and flats built to let'.[43] The ideological opposition to council housing from the 1980s onwards meant that it became marginalised, neglected and underfunded.

In 1976 the GLC had correctly assumed that approaches to housing would not remain static.[44] As it was then, so it is now: since climate change demands the retrofitting of ageing housing stock, and for all new buildings to be constructed to higher environmental standards, it is logical to reappraise council housing too. After all, as John Boughton points out, every form of council housing has been lauded by those who matter most – the people who lived in them – and many estates subsequently labelled as 'failed' were successful in their earlier years. Excepting some with particular construction flaws, very few were born bad.[45]

Council housing, often hidden in plain sight, is arguably the greatest gift that architects have bequeathed London. Just as importantly, it has contributed immeasurably to not only the architectural, but also the social fabric of the capital.

[1] Elain Harwood, *Hope Space and Brutalism* (New Haven and London: Yale University Press, 2015), p. 67.
[2] Laurence Ward, *The London County Council Bomb Damage Maps 1939–1945* (London: Thames & Hudson, 2015), pp. 32, 33.
[3] Owen Hatherley, *Red Metropolis* (London: Repeater, 2020), pp. 78–9.
[4] John Boughton, *Municipal Dreams* (London: Verso, 2018), p. 73.
[5] John Boughton, *Municipal Dreams*, p. 93.
[6] H.P. Trenton, 25 Years in Public Architecture, *The Architect*, May 1978, p. 38.
[7] John Boughton, *A History of Council Housing in 100 Estates* (London: RIBA Publishing, 2023), p. 141.
[8] Stefan Muthesius and Miles Glendinning, *Towers for the Welfare State* (Edinburgh: The Scottish Centre for Conservation Studies, 2017), p. 5.
[9] Judith Lever, *Home Sweet Home* (London: Academy Editions, 1976), p. 48.
[10] Walter Segal, Housing for London Boroughs, *Architectural Design*, November 1948, p. 232.
[11] Kenneth Powell, *Powell & Moya* (London: The Twentieth Century Society/English Heritage/RIBA Publishing, 2009), p. 1.
[12] John Boughton, *Municipal Dreams*, p. 104.
[13] Elain Harwood, *Hope Space and Brutalism*, p. 67.
[14] John Boughton, *Municipal Dreams*, p. 105.
[15] Editorial, *Architects' Journal*, 24 June 1954, p. 757.
[16] Elain Harwood, *Hope Space and Brutalism*, p. 68.
[17] John Partridge, Roehampton Housing, *Journal 9: Housing the Twentieth Century Nation* (London: The Twentieth Century Society, 2008), p. 116.
[18] Elain Harwood, George Finch Obituary, *The Guardian*, 27 February 2013.
[19] Lever, *Home Sweet Home*, p. 58.
[20] Ian Nairn, *Nairn's London* (London: Penguin 1966), p. 200.
[21] LCC Housing at Bermondsey, *Architects' Journal*, 17 November 1960, p. 715.
[22] Tidey Street Housing Scheme, *The Architect and Building News*, 12 April 1956, p. 361.
[23] Lever, *Home Sweet Home*, p. 63.
[24] Elizabeth Layton, *Building by Local Authorities* (London: George Allen & Unwin, 1961), p. 131.
[25] Elain Harwood, *Chamberlin, Powell & Bon* (London: The Twentieth Century Society/English Heritage/RIBA Publishing, 2011), p. 34.
[26] Borough of Bethnal Green, Report of the Housing Committee (Council Meeting Minutes, 26 July 1951).
[27] A.W. Cleeve Barr, *Public Authority Housing* (London: B.T. Batsford, 1958), p. 149.
[28] London Government Act 1963, Part IX, s.74(1).
[29] Mark Swenarton, *Cook's Camden: The Making of Modern Housing* (London: Lund Humphries, 2017), p. 31.
[30] London Borough of Islington, Report of the Housing Committee: Awards for Good Design in Housing 1980 (Council Agenda, 27 January 1981).
[31] London Borough of Islington, Report of the Housing Committee (Council Agenda, 20 June 1967).
[32] John Bancroft, Housing at Aberdeen Park, London N5, *Architects' Journal*, 10 October 1979, p. 744.
[33] Kate Macintosh in *Utopia London*, directed by Tom Cordell (Punchcard Pictures, 2010).
[34] Peter Rawstorne: Interview with Edward Hollamby, *RIBA Journal*, July 1965, p. 351.
[35] Stefan Muthesius & Miles Glendinning, *Tower for the Welfare State*, p. 139.
[36] John Grindrod, *Concretopia* (London: Old Street Publishing, 2013), p. 339.
[37] John Boughton, *A History of Council Housing in 100 Estates*, p. 181.
[38] *Croydon Official Guide 1971* (London: Croydon London Borough Council, 1971), p. 23.
[39] *GLC Architecture 1965/70* (London: Greater London Council, 1971), p. 12.
[40] Owen Hatherley, *A Guide to the New Ruins of Great Britain* (London: Verso, 2010), p. 327.
[41] Housing Act 1980, Chapter 51.
[42] John Boughton, *Municipal Dreams*, p. 173.
[43] *Conservative Party Election Manifesto* (London, 1951).
[44] Judith Lever, *Home Sweet Home*, p. 111.
[45] John Boughton, *A History of Council Housing in 100 Estates*, p. 250.

NORTH-EAST

1. Tower Hamlets

2. Newham

3. Barking and Dagenham

4. Havering

5. Hackney

6. Waltham Forest

7. Redbridge

8. Haringey

9. Enfield

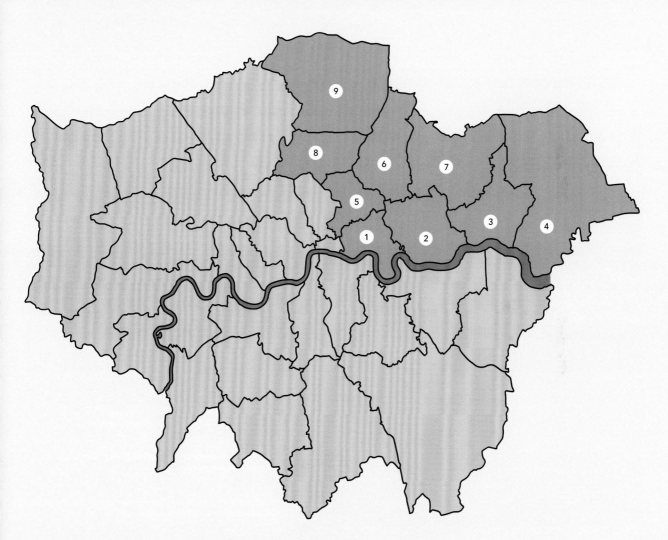

Top: Beecholme Estate, Prout Road, Hackney E5
Frederick Gibberd for Hackney Borough Council
1948–50

Bottom: 44 Gooshays Drive, Harold Hill Estate, Romford RM3
LCC Valuer's Department
1948

Right: 268–306 Tiverton Road, Tewkesbury Estate, Seven Sisters N15
Howes & Jackman for Tottenham Borough Council
1949

Baring House, Lansbury Estate, Poplar E14
LCC Architect's Department
1950–1

Cranston Estate, Hoxton N1
Lewis Solomon & Son for the LCC
Designed from 1948, built in 1951–2

Reynolds House, Approach Road Estate, Approach Road E2
Donald Hamilton, Wakeford & Partners for Bethnal Green Borough Council
1951–3

Hughes Mansions, Whitechapel E1
Stepney Engineer and Surveyor's Department
Borough engineer and surveyor: A.A. Hudson
Planned from 1946, approved in 1948, built in 1951–2

Ashdale House and Burtonwood House, Woodberry Down Estate, Manor House N4
LCC Architect's Department. Project architect: C.H. Walker
Designed from 1941, presented in 1943, built in 1952–3
Demolished

Balmoral House, Portland Rise Estate, Manor House N4
Howes & Jackman for Stoke Newington Borough Council
1952–4

Top: Longbridge Road, Barking IG11
Barking Corporation
Borough architect: C.C. Shaw
1952

Bottom: 19–36 Mount Pleasant, Mount Pleasant Estate, Ilford Lane IG1
Ilford Engineer's Department
Borough engineer: L.E.J. Reynolds
Assistant architect: H.B.N. Nixon
1955–6

Right: Falstaff House, Arden Estate, Hoxton N1
LCC Architect's Department
Designed from 1952, built in 1952–4

Vaine House and Granard House, Gascoyne Estate, Homerton E9
LCC Architect's Department
Project architect: C.G. Weald

Assistant architects: Colin St John Wilson, Peter J. Carter,
Alan Colquhoun, J.F. Metcalfe, A.H.R. Wetzel and I. Young
1952–4

Westhope House, Hereford Estate, Vallance Road E2
LCC Architect's Department
1956

Above: 31–40 Kebbell Terrace, Claremont Estate, Forest Gate E7
West Ham Architect's Department
Borough architect: Thomas E. North
1955–7

Right: Fife Road, Keir Hardie Estate, Canning Town E16
West Ham Architect's Department
Borough architect: Thomas E. North
1956

Behind: Ferrier Point
Newham Architect & Planning Officer's Department
Borough architect and planning officer: Thomas E. North
1966

Thorne House, St John's Estate, Isle of Dogs E14
Poplar Engineer and Surveyor's Department
Borough engineer and surveyor: W.J. Rankin
1956

Lakeview Estate, Old Ford Road, Victoria Park E3
Skinner, Bailey & Lubetkin for Bethnal Green Borough Council
1955–6

George Loveless House, Dorset Estate, Bethnal Green E2
Skinner, Bailey & Lubetkin for Bethnal Green Borough Council
1951–7

Left: Staircase in George Loveless House

Kerry House and Zion House, Sidney Street Estate, Stepney E1
Sydney Clough, Son & Partners for Stepney Borough Council
1954–7

Page 34: Sulkin House, Greenways Estate, Bethnal Green E2
Fry, Drew, Drake & Lasdun for Bethnal Green Borough Council
Project architect: Denys Lasdun. Assistant architect: Margaret Rodd
Designed in 1952–3, built in 1956–8
Grade II listed

Page 35: Keeling House, Claredale Street E2
Fry, Drew, Drake & Lasdun for Bethnal Green Borough Council
Project architect: Denys Lasdun
Designed in 1955, built in 1957–9
Grade II* listed

Yates House and Johnson House, Avebury Estate, Bethnal Green E2
LCC Architect's Department
1957–8

Storey House, St Matthias Estate, All Saints E14
LCC Architect's Department
1956–8

Windsor House, Greenways Estate, Bethnal Green E2
Yorke, Rosenberg & Mardall for Bethnal Green Borough Council
Designed in 1955, built in 1956–9

Rowley Gardens, Woodberry Down Estate, Manor House N4
LCC Architect's Department
1958–61

Parr Court, Wenlock Barn Estate, New North Road N1
Shoreditch Engineer, Surveyor and Architect's Department
Borough engineer, surveyor and architect: J.L. Sharratt
1958

29–71 Giraud Street and Talbot House, Lansbury Estate, Poplar E14
LCC Architect's Department
Designed from 1955, built in 1958–61

Castle Point, Boundary Road, Plaistow E13
Booth, Ledeboer & Pinckheard for West Ham Borough Council
1961–2

Sleaford House and Gayton House, Lincoln Estate, Bow E3
LCC Architect's Department
Project architect: A.J.M. Tolhurst
Designed from 1956, built in 1960–2

Odette Duval House, Clichy Estate, Smithy Street E1
Riches & Blythin for Stepney Borough Council
Planned from 1958, built in 1960–2

Gardner Close, Wanstead, Redbridge E11
Wates for Wanstead and Woodford Municipal Borough Council
Wates Architect's Department

Chief architect: Kenneth W. Bland
Project architects: Maurice Hardouin and Tony Whale
1962–5

Farnworth House, Manchester Estate, Isle of Dogs E14
LCC Architect's Department
1961–2

Market Parade and Leyton Green Tower, High Road, Leyton E10
Leyton Engineer and Surveyor's Department
Borough engineer and surveyor: G.K. Barker. Assistant architect: Albert S. Brickell
1961–2

Shoreditch House, Charles Square Estate, Old Street EC1
Shoreditch Engineer and Surveyor's Department
Borough engineer, surveyor and architect: J.L. Sharratt
1961–2

To the right: Shoreditch Fire Station
LCC Architect's Department
Project architects: A.R. Borrett and T.M. Williams
Designed from 1960, built in 1962–5

Kilbrennan House, Abberfeldy Estate, Poplar E14
Poplar Engineer and Surveyor's Department
Borough engineer and surveyor: W.J. Rankin
1963
Planned for demolition

Right: Benfleet Court, Haggerston East Estate, Haggerston E8
LCC Architect's Department
Project architect: George Finch
Designed from 1959, built in 1963–4

Durham Avenue and Elvet Avenue, Gidea Park RM2
Phases 1 and 2
Wates in association with the Romford Engineer and Surveyor's Department
Borough engineer and surveyor: Hugh Hurd

Deputy borough architect: Stanley Stewart
Wates Architect's Department
Chief architect: Kenneth W. Bland
1963–6

Gooch House, Kenninghall Road, Clapton E5
Co-operative Planning Ltd for Hackney Borough Council
Designed from 1960, built in 1962–3

Graham House, Goodwin Road, Edmonton N11
Edmonton Architect and Planning Officer's Department
Borough architect: T.A. Wilkinson
1962–3

Behind: Walbrook House
Enfield Architect and Planning Officer's Department
Borough architect and planning officer: T.A. Wilkinson
1967–8

Chudleigh Street and Latham House, Mountmorres Estate,
Stepney E1
LCC Architect's Department
Project architect: A.C.H. Boyd
1960–3

Kingward House, Chicksand Estate, Whitechapel E1
LCC Architect's Department
Project architect: George Finch
Designed from 1958, completed by the GLC Department
of Architecture and Civic Design in 1967

Right: Pauline House and Spring Walk, Chicksand Estate,
Whitechapel E1
LCC Architect's Department
Project architect: George Finch
Designed from 1958, built in 1962–3

John Keats House, Commerce Road Estate, Wood Green N22
Wood Green Engineer's Department
Borough engineer: A.J. Rebbeck
Planned from 1958, built in 1963–4

page 58: Wayman Court, Eleanor Road, London Fields E8
Co-operative Planning Ltd for Hackney Borough Council
1964

page 59: Fred Wigg Tower, Montague Estate, Leytonstone E11
Leyton Engineer and Surveyor's Department
Borough architect and surveyor: G.K. Barker.
Assistant architect: Albert S. Brickell
1962–5

Douglas Road and Kildare Road, Canning Town E16
Development Group of the Ministry of Housing and Local Government (project architects: A.W. Cleeve-Barr and Oliver Cox) in association with the West Ham Architect's Department (borough architect: Thomas E. North) 1961–4

Cranbrook Estate, Mace Street, Bethnal Green E2
Skinner, Bailey & Lubetkin for Bethnal Green Borough Council
Designed from 1955, built in 1960–5

Right: Staircase in Offenbach House, Cranbrook Estate

Fletcher House and Chaucer Court, Milton Gardens Estate, Howard Road N16
Howes & Jackman for Stoke Newington Borough Council
1964

Laburnum House, Becontree Heath Estate, Wood Lane RM10
Barking Architect's Department
Borough architect: Matthew Maybury
1965

Hathaway Crescent, Shakespeare Crescent, East Ham E12
East Ham Engineer and Surveyor's Department
Borough engineer and surveyor: F.C. Ball
Designed from 1963, built and completed for Newham London Borough Council in 1966

Chalkwell House, Pitsea Estate, Commercial Road E1
A. & N. Moffett for the LCC
Designed from 1963, completed for the GLC in 1966

Melford Court, Melford Court Estate, Upper Clapton Road E5
Co-operative Planning Ltd for Hackney London Borough Council
1966

Sara Lane Court, Harman Street Estate, Kingsland Road N1
Hackney Architect's Department
Borough architect: J.L. Sharratt
1966

Kipling Towers and Dryden Towers, Heaton Avenue, Romford RM3
Havering Architect's Department
Borough architect: D. Pearcy
1966

Sivill House, Dorset Estate, Columbia Road E2
Skinner, Bailey & Lubetkin for Bethnal Green Council
Designed from 1960, completed for Tower Hamlets London Borough Council in 1966
Grade II listed

Balfron Tower, Brownfield Estate, Poplar E14
Ernő Goldfinger for the GLC
Designed in 1963–4 for the LCC, built in 1965–8
Grade II* listed

Glenkerry House (1972–5, Grade II listed), Carradale House (1967–8, Grade II listed) and
Balfron Tower (1965–8, Grade II* listed, after refurbishment), Brownfield Estate, Poplar E14
Ernő Goldfinger for the LCC and GLC

Top: A decorative screen at Norwich House, Lansbury Estate, Poplar E14
LCC Architect's Department
Design consultant: William Mitchell
Designed from 1955, built in 1959–61

Bottom: Wall-mounted aluminium sculpture at Elmslie Point, Leopold Estate, Mile End E3
LCC Architect's Department
Design consultant: Anthony Hollaway
1967

Left: Elmslie Point, Leopold Estate, Mile End E3
LCC Architect's Department
Designed from 1962, built for the GLC in 1965–7

Haberdasher Estate, Haberdasher Street, Hoxton N1
Stock, Page & Stock for Hackney London Borough Council
1966–7

Right: Lewey House, Bede Estate, Mile End E3
Riches & Blythin for Stepney Borough Council
Commissioned in 1964, built and completed for Tower Hamlets
London Borough Council in 1966–7

Hedley House, Samuda Estate, Isle of Dogs E14
Sir John Burnet, Tait & Partners for the LCC
Project architect: Gordon Tait
Planned and designed from 1964, built for the GLC in 1965–7

Kelson House, Samuda Estate, Isle of Dogs E14
Sir John Burnet, Tait & Partners for the LCC
Project architect: Gordon Tait
Planned and designed from 1964, built for the GLC in 1965–7

Wyndham Deedes House, St Peter's Estate, Hackney Road E2
Co-operative Planning Ltd for Bethnal Green Borough Council
Commissioned in 1962, completed for Tower Hamlets London Borough Council in 1967

Arthur Walls House, Grantham Road, Little Ilford E12
East Ham Borough Engineer and Surveyor's Department
Borough engineer and surveyor: F.C. Ball
Designed from 1963, built for Newham London Borough Council in 1967–8

Top: Lund Point and Doran Walk, Carpenters Estate, Stratford E15
Newham Architect and Planning Officer's Department
Borough architect and planner: Thomas E. North.
Assistant architect: Kenneth Lund
First design in 1963 by West Ham Architect's Department under North, built in 1965-8

Bottom: 339-428 Fellows Court, Fellows Court Estate, Hoxton E2
Shoreditch Engineer and Surveyor's Department
Borough engineer, surveyor and architect: J.L. Sharratt
1963

Opposite
Top left: Mersea House and Colne House, Harts Lane Estate, Barking IG11
Barking Architect's Department
Borough architect: Matthew Maybury
1968

Top right: Corbiere House and Granville Court (1966), Rozel Court (1965) and Portelet Court (1968), De Beauvoir Estate, Haggerston N1
Burley Associates for Hackney Borough Council
Designed from 1963, completed for Hackney London Borough Council in 1975

Bottom left: Curlew House, Merlin House and Cormorant House, Alma Estate, Ponders End EN3
Enfield Architect and Planning Officer's Department
Borough architect and planning officer: T.A. Wilkinson
1966-8
Planned for demolition

Bottom right: Sunset Court, Orchard Estate, Broadmead Road, Woodford IG8
E.D. Mills & Partners for Redbridge London Borough Council
1966-8

Darnley House, Limehouse Fields Estate, Limehouse E14
Caledonia House and Anglia House, Brunton Wharf Estate
Tower Hamlets Architect's Department
Borough architect: John D. Hume
1966–9

Bow Cross/Crossways Estate, Bow Road E3
GLC Department of Architecture and Civic Design
1968–70

Imperial Wharf Estate, Craven Park Road, Stamford Hill N15
Haringey Department of Architecture
Borough architect: Charles E. Jacob. Job architect: Janina Chodakowska
1970–1

Right: Tangmere, Broadwater Farm Estate, Tottenham N17
Haringey Department of Architecture
Borough architect: Charles E. Jacob. Deputy borough architect: Alan Weitzel
Designed from 1966, built in 1967–72
Demolished

Oban House and Wheelers Cross, Gascoigne Estate, Barking IG11
Barking Architect's Department
Borough architect: Matthew Maybury
1970–2

Charles Dickens House, Mansford Estate, Bethnal Green E2
Tower Hamlets Architect's Department
Borough architect: John D. Hume
1967–9

North Square, Edmonton Green, Enfield N9
Enfield Borough Architect and Planning Officer's Department
Borough architect and planning officer: T.A. Wilkinson
1970–2

Stockholm House, Hatton House and Shearsmith House, St George's Estate, Cable Street E1
LCC Architect's Department
Project architect: George Finch
Designed from 1964, built by the GLC Department of Architecture and Civic Design in 1968–72

105–214 Robin Hood Gardens, Robin Hood Gardens, Poplar E14
Alison and Peter Smithson for the GLC
Designed in 1966–70, built in 1968–72
Demolition started in 2017

Right: 105–214 Robin Hood Gardens, Floor 8

Right: 35–59 Market Square, Lansbury Estate, Chrisp Street E14
GLC Department of Architecture and Civic Design
Designed from 1967, built in 1971–3

Behind: The Chrisp Street Market clock tower
Frederick Gibberd; 1951–2
Grade II listed

Fitzgerald House, Lansbury Estate, Chrisp Street E14
GLC Department of Architecture and Civic Design
1968–71

Crondall Street 244–78, Arden Estate, Hoxton N1
Leonard Manasseh & Partners for the GLC
Designed from 1968, built in 1972–4

Helston Court, Russell Road, South Tottenham N15
John Melvin & Partners for Haringey London Borough Council
1974

Kedleston Walk, Teesdale Estate, Bethnal Green E2
Douglas Stephen & Partners for the GLC
1972–4

Russell Road Estate, Russell Road, South Tottenham N15
Howell Killick Partridge & Amis for Haringey London Borough Council
Partner in charge: John Partridge
1971–81

Ashington House, Collingwood Estate, Whitechapel E1
Noel Moffett & Associates for the GLC
1971–5
Planned for demolition

Morant Place, Commerce Road, Wood Green N22
Ivor Smith & Cailey Hutton for Haringey London Borough Council
1975

Fairlie Court, Stroudley Walk, Bow Bridge Estate, Bromley-by-Bow E3
GLC Department of Architecture and Civic Design
1979–82

Burr Close, South Quay Plaza Estate, St Katharine Docks E1
Renton Howard Wood Associates for the GLC
1975–7

Ferry Lane Estate, Tottenham Hale N17
GLC Department of Architecture and Civic Design
Project architect: Jack Lambert
Designed from 1970, revised plans from 1972, built in 1977–81

Wyemead Crescent, Friday Hill Estate, Chingford E4
GLC Department of Architecture and Civic Design
1973–7

NORTH-WEST

1. City of London

2. City of Westminster

3. Kensington and Chelsea

4. Hammersmith and Fulham

5. Hounslow

6. Richmond upon Thames

7. Ealing

8. Brent

9. Camden

10. Islington

11. Hillingdon

12. Harrow

13. Barnet

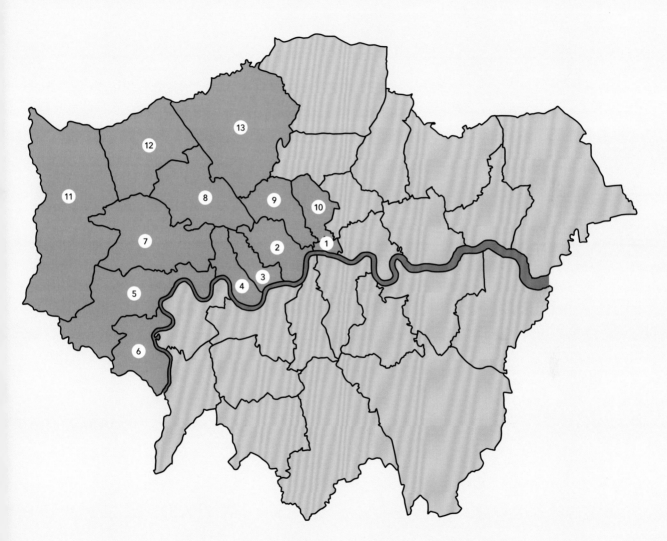

Top: Aubert Court, Highbury N5
E.C.P. Monson for Islington Borough Council
1946–53

Bottom: Fleming Court, St Mary's Square, Paddington W2
Paddington Engineer's Department
Borough engineer: A.L. Downey
Planned from 1945, built in 1947–8
Opened on 2 October 1948 by Alexander Fleming

Right: Blemundsbury, Tybalds Close Estate, Boswell Street, Holborn
Hening & Chitty for Holborn Borough Council
Approved in 1946, designed in 1947–8, completed in 1949

Whitley House and Moyle House, Churchill Gardens Estate, Pimlico SW1
Powell & Moya for Westminster City Council
1957–62

Right: Blackstone House, Churchill Gardens Estate, Pimlico SW1
Powell & Moya for Westminster City Council
1952–7

Coleridge House, Churchill Gardens Estate, Pimlico SW1
Powell & Moya for Westminster City Council
Competition-winning design from 1946, built in 1948–51
Grade II listed

Sadler House, Spa Green Estate, Islington EC1
Tecton for Finsbury Borough Council
After dissolution of Tecton completed by executive architects Skinner & Lubetkin
Designed from 1938, redesigned in 1943, built in 1946–9
Grade II* listed

Wells House, Spa Green Estate, Islington EC1
Tecton for Finsbury Borough Council
After dissolution of Tecton completed by executive architects Skinner & Lubetkin
Designed from 1938, redesigned in 1943, built in 1946–9
Grade II* listed

Newbury House, Hallfield Estate, Paddington W2
Tecton for Paddington Borough Council
After dissolution of Tecton completed by executive architects Drake & Lasdun
Designed in 1946–8, built in 1949–55
Grade II listed

Right: Exeter House and Winchester House, Hallfield Estate, Paddington W2

Kendal House, Priory Green Estate, and Priory Heights, King's Cross N1
Tecton for Finsbury Borough Council
After dissolution of Tecton completed by executive architects Skinner, Bailey & Lubetkin
Designed from 1943, redesigned in 1947, built in 1948–57

Griesdale, Regent's Park Estate, Regent's Park NW1
Davies & Arnold for St Pancras Borough Council
1953

Parmoor Court, Stafford Cripps Estate, Clerkenwell EC1
Joseph Emberton for Finsbury Borough Council
1953–6

Barrington Court, Barrington and Lamble Estate, Gospel Oak NW5
Powell & Moya for St Pancras Borough Council
1952–4

Left: Staircase in Bevin Court, Cruikshank Street, Islington WC1
Tecton for Finsbury Borough Council
After dissolution of Tecton completed by executive architects Skinner
Bailey & Lubetkin
Designed from 1946, present design from 1949, built in 1951–4
Grade II* listed

Right: Holford House, Bevin Court, Cruikshank Street, Islington WC1

Buckland House, Abbots Manor Estate, Pimlico SW1
Riches & Blythin for Westminster City Council
1952–5

Gorefield House, South Kilburn Estate, Gorefield Place NW6
Arthur M. Foyle for Willesden Borough Council
1954

The Grange, Lytton Estate, Lisgar Terrace W14
Fulham Architect's Department
Borough architect: J. Pritchard Lovell
1960–3

Jim Griffiths House, Clem Attlee Estate, Fulham SW6
Fulham Architect's Department
Borough architect: J. Pritchard Lovell
1955–7

Glover House, Harben Estate, Swiss Cottage NW6
Norman & Dawbarn for Hampstead Borough Council
1954–5

Haslam House, Newbery Estate, Essex Road N1
LCC Architect's Department
1955

Bowater House (1953–6) and Great Arthur House (1953–7), Golden Lane Estate, Golden Lane EC1
Chamberlin, Powell & Bon for Corporation of London
A competition-winning design by Geoffry Powell from 1952, built to revised design by Chamberlin, Powell & Bon
Grade II listed

Basterfield House, Golden Lane Estate, Golden Lane EC1
1954–6
Grade II listed

Right: Crescent House (1958–62, Grade II* listed) and Hatfield House (1958–61, Grade II listed), Golden Lane Estate

13–56 Norfolk Close, East Finchley N2
I.R. Southcombe for Finchley Borough Council
1959

Farjeon House, Hilgrove Estate, Swiss Cottage NW6
LCC Architect's Department
1958

11–90 Kilburn Square, Kilburn High Road NW6
Co-operative Planning Ltd for Willesden Borough Council
1961–4

Kiln Place, Kiln Place Estate, Gospel Oak NW5
Armstrong & MacManus for St Pancras Borough Council
Project architect: Brian Smith
1957–62

Midford House, Belle Vue Estate, Hendon NW4
Hendon Engineer and Surveyor's Department
Borough engineer and surveyor: J.L. Pelham
Chief architect: P.J. Whittle
1963

Chancellors Court, Tybalds Close Estate, Holborn WC1
Holborn Architect's Department
Borough architect and director of housing: Sydney Cook
1959–61

Top: Braithwaite House, Bunhill Row EC1
LCC Architect's Department
1963–4

Bottom: Crone Court, South Kilburn Estate, South Kilburn NW6
Willesden Architect's Department
Borough architect: Thomas N. I'Anson
1963–4

Opposite
Top left: 45–88 Upper Fosters, Fosters Estate, Hendon NW4
Hendon Engineer and Surveyor's Department
Borough engineer and surveyor: J.L. Pelham
1958–9

Top right: William Blake House, Dufour's Place, Soho W1
Stillman & Eastwick-Field for Westminster City Council
1964–6

Bottom left: Bourne Terrace, Warwick Estate, Paddington W2
LCC Architect's Department
Planned and designed from 1954, built in 1963–5

Bottom right: Malabar Court, White City Estate, India Way,
Shepherd's Bush W12
Noel Moffett & Associates for the GLC
1966

Michael Cliffe House and Patrick Coman House, Finsbury Estate, Finsbury EC1
Emberton, Franck & Tardrew for Finsbury Borough Council
Commissioned in 1961, built and completed by Franck & Deeks for Islington London Borough Council
1965–7

Michael Cliffe House, Finsbury Estate, mosaic

Gaymead and Mary Green, Abbey Estate, South Hampstead NW8
J.M. Austin-Smith and Partners in association with the Hampstead Engineer and Surveyor's Department
Hampstead housing architect: Charles E. Jacob
Designed from 1963, built for London Camden Borough Council in 1966–8

Fairchild House and Henry Wise House, Lillington Gardens Estate, Pimlico SW1
Darbourne & Darke for Westminster City Council
A competition-winning design by John Darbourne from 1961, detailed and built by Darbourne & Darke in 1964–7
Grade II* listed

Hartopp Point, Aintree Estate, Dawes Road, Fulham SW6
GLC Department of Architecture and Civic Design
Based on the original design for the Morris Walk Estate by project
architects Martin Richardson, George Bailey and Ronald Parker

1968–70
Demolished

Left: Playground, Aintree Estate

Colinsdale, Camden Passage, Angel N1
E.C.P. Monson in association with the Islington Architect's Department
Borough architect: Alf Head
1967–9

Right: Lampeter Square, Bayonne Estate, Fulham W6
GLC Department of Architecture and Civic Design
1968

Tremlett Grove Estate, Upper Holloway N19
GLC Department of Architecture and Civic Design
1967–8

Grange Farm Estate, Shaftesbury Avenue, South Harrow HA2
Harrow Department of Architecture and Planning
Borough architect: Geoffrey J. Foxley
1969
Planned for demolition

Kestrel House, Kestrel House Estate, City Road EC1
Franck & Deeks for Islington London Borough Council
1968–9

Caldy Walk, Marquess Estate, Canonbury N1
Darbourne & Darke for Islington London Borough Council
1966–76
Remodelled by Shepheard Epstein Hunter (1979) and Islington Architects (1998–2002)

Elsfield, Highgate Road, Kentish Town NW5
Camden Architect's Department
Borough architect: Sydney Cook
Project architect: Bill Forrest
Designed in 1967, built in 1968–70

Sheldon House, Cromwell Road, Teddington TW11
Manning & Clamp for Richmond upon Thames London Borough Council
1969
Planned for demolition

Right: Petticoat Square, Middlesex Street Estate, Aldgate E1
Corporation of London Department of Architecture & Planning
City architect: E.G. Chandler
1967–9

Hathersage Court, Newington Green N1
Co-operative Planning Ltd for Islington London Borough Council
1970–1

Right: Harlech Tower, South Acton Estate, Acton W3
Ealing Architect's Department
Borough architect: Thomas N. l'Anson
1968–70

Slide structure in children's playground, Brunel Estate,
Great Western Road W2
Michael Brown for Westminster City Council
1973–4, Grade II listed

Right: Spring Gardens, Highbury New Park, Islington N5
Islington Architect's Department
Borough architect: Alf Head
1968–70

Hayes Town Centre Estate, Hayes UB3
Hillingdon Architect's Department
Borough architect: Thurston Williams
1971
Planned for demolition

Tideswell, Ingestre Road Estate, Tufnell Park NW5
Camden Architect's Department
Borough architect: Sydney Cook
Project architect: John Green
Designed in 1965–6, built in 1969–71

Rutherford Tower and Wallis Road, Mount Pleasant Estate, Southall UB1
Ealing Architect's Department
Borough architect: Thomas N. l'Anson
1968–71

Stock Orchard Estate, Stock Orchard Crescent, Holloway N7
Sir Basil Spence OM RA for Islington London Borough Council
1970–1

Foundling Court, Brunswick Centre, Bloomsbury WC1
Patrick Hodgkinson for Marchmont Properties and Camden London Borough Council
Designed with Leslie Martin in 1960–3, subsequent scheme 1963–8
Built in 1968–72, Grade II listed

Lowerwood Court, Convent Estate, Ladbroke Grove W11
Royal Borough of Kensington and Chelsea Architect's Department
Borough architect: F.L. Willars
1970–2

Longleat House and Thorndike House, Lillington Gardens Estate, Pimlico SW1
Darbourne & Darke for Westminster City Council
A competition-winning design by John Darbourne from 1961, detailed by Darbourne & Darke
The third phase of the scheme, Lillington 3, built in 1969–72
Grade II listed

Demolition of Gloucester House in 2018, South Kilburn Estate NW6

Blake Court and Dickens House, South Kilburn Estate NW6
Brent Architect's Department
Borough architect: A.G. Beckett
1971–3
Planned for demolition

Trellick Tower, Trellick & Edenham, Cheltenham Estate, North Kensington W10
Ernő Goldfinger for the GLC; 1968–72
Grade II* listed
Above: Reception in Trellick Tower

Far left: Braithwaite Tower, Paddington Green Estate W2
Paddington Architect's Department
Borough architect and director of housing: W.H. Beesley
Planned from 1957, designed in 1962–3, built in 1964–5

Centre: Kennet House, Church Street Area NW8
Bridgwater and Shepheard for St Marylebone Borough Council
1957–9

Front: Cherwell House, Church Street Area NW8
Easton & Robertson for St Marylebone Borough Council
Planned and designed from 1944, built in 1946–50

Right: Ashcroft Square, King Street, Hammersmith W6
R. Seifert & Partners in association with the Hammersmith Architect's
Department
Borough architect and planning officer: E.G. Sames
1973

Top: Northampton Park, Canonbury N1
Darbourne & Darke for Islington Borough Council
1971–3

Bottom: Keighley Close, Camden Road, Holloway N7
Darbourne & Darke for Islington London Borough Council
Designed from 1969, built in 1972–3

Opposite
Top left: Legion Close, Offord Road, Highbury N1
Islington Architect's Department
Borough architect: Alf Head
1972–4

Top right: Harford House, Tavistock Crescent Estate,
Westbourne Park W11
Westminster Department of Architecture and Planning
Borough architect: J.M. Hirsch
Project architect: Maxwell Stewart
1972–5

Bottom left: Swinbrook Estate, North Kensington W10
GLC Department of Architecture and Civic Design
1973–5

Bottom right: Wessex Gardens Estate, St Stephen's Gardens,
Notting Hill W11
Westminster Department of Architecture and Planning
Borough architect: J.M. Hirsch
1975

Shelbourne House and Iberia House, New Orleans Estate, Hornsey Lane N19
Islington Architect's Department
Borough architect: Alf Head
1971–4

Right: Church Street Estate, Church Street Area, Marylebone NW8
Westminster Department of Architecture and Planning
Borough architect: F.G. West
1968–75
Awaiting demolition

1–107 Woodhall, Robert Street, Camden NW1
Frederick MacManus & Partners for Camden London Borough Council
1970–5

Maiden Lane Estate, York Way NW1
Camden Architect's Department
Borough architects/Directors of architecture: Sydney Cook (1965–73) and Alfred Rigby (1973–8)
Project architects: Gordon Benson and Alan Forsyth
Designed from 1972, presented in 1975, built 1976–82

Midway House, Earlstoke Estate, Goswell Road EC1
Renton Howard Wood Associates for the GLC
Designed in 1969–70, built in 1972–6

Girdlestone Estate, Archway N19
Islington Architect's Department
Borough architect: Alf Head
1975–6

Oakshott Court, Polygon Road, Somers Town NW1
Borough architects/Directors of architecture: Sydney Cook (1965–73)
and Alfred Rigby (1973–8)
Project architect: Peter Tábori (succeeded by Roman Halter, 1971–4
and James Gowan, 1974–6)
Designed in 1969–71, completed in 1976

Westbourne Estate, Holloway N7
Eric Lyons, Cadbury-Brown, Metcalfe and Cunningham Group Partnership
for Islington London Borough Council
1974–6

Right: Berenger Tower, World's End Estate, Chelsea SW10
Eric Lyons, Cadbury-Brown, Metcalfe and Cunningham for Chelsea
Borough Council
Partner in charge: John Metcalfe
Project architect: Oliver West
Commissioned in 1963, built for Kensington and Chelsea London
Borough Council in 1969–77

Dunboyne Road Estate, Gospel Oak NW3
Camden Architect's Department
Borough architects/Directors of architecture: Sydney Cook (1965-73) and Alfred Rigby (1973-8)
Project architect: Neave Brown
Designed in 1966–7, built in 1971–7, Grade II listed

Dudley Court, Covent Garden WC2
Powell & Moya for Camden London Borough Council
1973–83

Behind: Oasis Sports Centre
Holborn Architect's Department
Borough architect: Sydney Cook
Designed from 1957, built in 1959–61

Highgrove Estate, Ruislip Manor HA4
Edward Cullinan Architects for Hillingdon London Borough Council
Designed from 1974, built in 1977–8

Spedan Close, Hampstead NW3
Camden Architect's Department
Borough architects/Directors of architecture: Sydney Cook (1965–73) and Alfred Rigby (1973–8)
Project architects: Gordon Benson and Alan Forsyth
Designed from 1971, built in 1974–8, Grade II listed

Sandstone Place, Whittington Estate, Archway N19
Camden Architect's Department
Borough architects/Directors of architecture: Sydney Cook (1965–73) and Alfred Rigby (1973–9)
Project architect: Peter Tábori
Designed from 1968, built in 1972–9

Block A, Rowley Way, Alexandra & Ainsworth Estate, South Hampstead NW8
Camden Architect's Department
Borough architects/Directors of architecture: Sydney Cook (1965–73), Alfred Rigby (1973–8)
Project architect: Neave Brown
Designed in 1967–9, built in 1972–9 Grade II* listed

Crabtree Wharf Estate, Crabtree Lane, Hammersmith SW6
Hammersmith and Fulham Architect's Department
Borough architect: J.S. Campbell
Project architect: Anthony Warren
1978

Right: Perran Walk, Haverfield Estate, Brentford TW8
Hounslow Architect's Department
Borough architect: G.A. Trevett
1974–9

Wood Lane Estate, White City W12
Darbourne & Darke for Hammersmith London Borough Council
1975–8

Hermes Walk, Smiths Farm Estate, Northolt UB5
GLC Department of Architecture and Civic Design
1972–9

Whitbread Centre, Whitecross Street EC1
Fitzroy Robinson & Partners for Islington London Borough Council
Designed from 1975 for Whitbread & Co.
Transferred to Islington London Borough Council and completed in 1982

Mansfield Road, Gospel Oak NW3
Camden Architect's Department
Borough architects/Directors of architecture: Sydney Cook (1965–73),
Alfred Rigby (1973–9), John Green (acting, 1979–80)
Project architects: Gordon Benson and Alan Forsyth
Presented in 1972, built in 1974–80

Broadfield Lane, Maiden Lane Estate, York Way NW1
Camden Architect's Department
Directors of architecture: Alfred Rigby (1973–9) and John Green
(acting, 1979–81)
Project architect for Stage II: Daniel Usiskin
Original design for Stage I by Gordon Benson and Alan Forsyth
Designed in 1976, built in 1978–83

Right: Loudon Road housing, shops and craft workshops,
South Hampstead NW8
Tom Kay Associates for Camden London Borough Council
Designed in 1972–5, completed in 1980
Grade II listed

Seaforth Crescent, Aberdeen Park, Highbury N5
Darbourne & Darke for Islington London Borough Council
1979–80

Odhams Walk, Covent Garden WC2
GLC Department of Architecture and Civic Design
Group leader: Donald Ball. Project architect: M.B. O'Conner
1979–81

SOUTH-EAST

1. Southwark
2. Lewisham
3. Greenwich
4. Bexley
5. Bromley

Queen Adelaide Court, St John's Road, Penge SE20
Edward Armstrong for Penge Urban District Council
1951
Festival of Britain Award for Merit

Passfields, Bromley Road, Bellingham SE6
Fry, Drew and Partners for Lewisham Metropolitan Borough Council
Architect in charge: J.B. Shaw
1949–51
Festival of Britain Award for Merit, Grade II listed

Top: Worsley House, Shackleton Close Estate, Forest Hill SE23
Lewisham Borough Architect's Department
Borough architect: M.H. Forward. Assistant architect: J.F. Kennedy
1951

Bottom: Lamas Green Estate, Sydenham Hill, Forest Hill SE26
Farquharson and McMorran for Corporation of London
Architect in charge: Donald McMorran
1955–7
Grade II listed

Opposite
Top left: Maitland Close, Maitland Close Estate,
Greenwich High Road SE10
Greenwich Engineer and Surveyor's Department
Borough engineer and surveyor: F.H. Clinch
Chief architect: P.A. Kennedy
1956–8

Top right: Tomson House and Thetford House, St Saviours Estate,
Abbey Street, Bermondsey SE1
Clifford Culpin & Partner for Bermondsey Borough Council
1958

Bottom left: Lawson Estate, Great Dover Street, Southwark SE1
Sir John Burnet, Tait & Partners for the LCC
Planned and designed from 1951, built in 1956–7

Bottom right: 164–202 Panfield Road, Abbey Wood Estate,
Abbey Wood SE2
LCC Architect's Department
Architect in charge: H.J.W. Broadwater
Project architect: S.B. Mendelsohn
1960

20–46 Rosamond Street, Dallas & Springfield Estate, Sydenham SE26
LCC Architect's Department
Designed from 1954, built in 1958

Forbes House, Woodland Road Estate, Gipsy Hill SE19
Camberwell Architect's Department
Borough architect: F.O. Hayes
1958

John Kennedy House and Brydale House, Hawkstone Estate, Rotherhithe New Road SE16
LCC Architect's Department
Architect in charge: Edward Hollamby. Project architect: Irma Stypulkowska
1958–62

Lakanal House, Sceaux Gardens Estate, Camberwell SE5
Camberwell Architect's Department
Borough architect: F.O. Hayes. Deputy borough architect: H.C. Connell. Project architect: H.P. Trenton
1957–9

Offham House, Congreve Estate, Walworth SE17
G.E. Skeats for Southwark Borough Council
1962–3

Right: Brandon Estate, Kennington SE17
LCC Architect's Department
Architect in charge: Edward Hollamby
Presented in 1955, built in 1957–61

Prospect House, Gaywood Estate, Elephant and Castle SE1
LCC Architect's Department
1962

32–108 Dartford Street, Gateway Estate, Walworth SE17
LCC Architect's Department
1960–2

1–69 Becton Place, Erith, Bexley DA8
Erith Engineer and Surveyor's Department
Borough engineer and surveyor: John H. Clayton
1962

Foreground: Heston House, Tanners Hill Estate, Deptford SE8
LCC Valuer's Department
1946

Centre: Pitman House, Tanners Hill Estate
LCC Architect's Department
1964

Eardley Point, Armstrong Estate, Woolwich SE18
LCC Architect's Department
Designed in 1962, built in 1964

Nayland House, Watermead Estate, Bromley Road, Bellingham SE6
LCC Architect's Department
1963

Right: Hillcrest Estate, High Level Drive, Sydenham SE26
LCC Architect's Department
1962–3

Frederick House, Morris Walk Estate, Prospect Vale SE7
LCC Architect's Department
Project architects: Martin Richardson, George Bailey and Ronald Parker
Designed from 1962, built in 1964–6
Planned for demolition

Westcombe Court and Combe Avenue, Vanbrugh Park Estate, Blackheath SE3
Chamberlin, Powell & Bon for Greenwich Borough Council
Designed from 1959, built in 1961–4

Walpole Place, Woolwich SE18
LCC Architect's Department
Designed from 1961, built in 1964

Tabard Gardens Estate, Tabard Street, Southwark SE1
Skinner, Bailey & Lubetkin for the LCC
Designed in 1963–4, built in 1965

Sidmouth House, Lindley Estate, Lympstone Gardens SE15
LCC Architect's Department
Designed from 1960, built by the GLC Department of Architecture and Civic Design in 1966

Hill Beck Close 'old people's home & flatlets', Tustin Estate, Old Kent Road SE15
Sir Basil Spence, Bonnington & Collins for the LCC
1965
Planned for demolition

Argosy House and, behind, Aragon Tower and Daubeney Tower, Pepys Estate, Deptford SE8
LCC Architect's Department
Designed from 1963, completed by the GLC Department of Architecture and Civic Design in 1973

Riverside Youth Club
Pepys Estate, Deptford SE8
GLC Department of Architecture and Civic Design
1968

Lambrook House, Clifton Estate, Peckham SE15
LCC Architect's Department
Designed from 1961, built by the GLC Department of Architecture and Civic Design in 1967–70

Bowling Green Row, St Mary's Estate, Woolwich SE18
Woolwich Borough Engineer and Surveyor's Department
Borough engineer and surveyor: Robert L. Gee
Borough architect: John M. Moore
Designed from 1961, built by the Greenwich Architect's Department 1965–8

Coralline Walk, Lesnes, Thamesmead SE28
GLC Department of Architecture and Civic Design
Divisional architect: Robert Rigg
Project architects: Philip Bottomley, Norman Engleback, J.A. Roberts, John Knight, G.A. Comrie-Smith and P.A. Westwood
Planned from 1963 by the LCC Architect's Department, master plan by the GLC Department of Architecture and Civic Design approved in 1967, built in 1967–8
Demolished

Right: Binsey Walk, Southmere, Thamesmead SE28
GLC Department of Architecture and Civic Design
1967–8
Demolished

Webb Court, Keynes Court and Lytton Strachey Path, Moorings,
Thamesmead SE28
GLC Department of Architecture and Civic Design
Thamesmead manager: Geoffrey Horsfall

Project architect: Stephen Mooring
Consulting architects: Gollins Melvin Ward & Partners
Designed from 1971, built in 1972–7

Trewsbury House, Penton House and Osney House, Southmere,
Thamesmead SE28
GLC Department of Architecture and Civic Design
1967–8

Top: Arnot House, Wyndham & Comber Estate, Camberwell SE5
GLC Department of Architecture and Civic Design
1967

Bottom: The Jessie Duffett Hall, Wyndham & Comber Estate,
Camberwell SE5
LCC Architect's Department
Architect in charge: Colin Lucas. Project architect: Philip Bottomley
Designed from 1962, approved in 1964, completed by the GLC Department
of Architecture and Civic Design in 1968

Right: Otterburn House and Crossmount House, Wyndham & Comber
Estate, Camberwell SE5
1968

Polthorne Estate, Plumstead SE18
Lyons Israel & Ellis
Designed for the LCC from 1963, built for the GLC in 1965–9

Right: Lupin House, Dickens Estate, Bermondsey SE16
LCC Architect's Department
Designed from 1962, completed by the GLC Department of Architecture
and Civic Design in 1969

Lapwing Tower and Guillemot Court, Evelyn Estate, Deptford SE8
Lewisham Architect's Department
Borough architect: M.H. Forward
1967–9

Winslow and Wendover 241–471, Aylesbury Estate, Walworth SE17
Southwark Development Department
Director of development: Ceri Griffiths
Borough architect: H.P. Trenton
1974–6
Planned for demolition

Right: Taplow 1–215, Aylesbury Estate, Walworth SE17
Southwark Department of Architecture and Planning
Borough architect and planner: F.O. Hayes
Deputy borough architect and planner: H.P. Trenton
Project architect: Derek Winch
1967–70
Planned for demolition

Ledbury Estate, Commercial Way, Peckham SE15
GLC Department of Architecture and Civic Design
Based on the original design for the Morris Walk Estate by project architects
Martin Richardson, George Bailey and Ronald Parker
1968–70
Planned for demolition

Tissington Court, Silverlock Estate, Rotherhithe SE16
Stock, Page & Stock for Bermondsey Borough Council
Designed from 1963, built for Southwark London Borough Council in 1967–70

Right: Dawson's Heights, Dawson's Hill, East Dulwich SE22
Southwark Department of Architecture & Planning
Borough architect: F.O. Hayes
Project architect: Kate Macintosh
1966–72

Top: Coxson Way, Fair Community, Druid Street SE1
Peter Moro & Partners for Southwark London Borough Council
1969–75

Bottom: Hamilton Square, Kipling Street, London Bridge SE1
Peter Moro & Partners for Southwark London Borough Council
1969–73

Right: Carrack House, Saltforth Close, Erith DA8
R. Seifert & Partners in association with the Bexley Architect's Department
Borough architect: Roy Thornley
1967–71

Edge Hill, Woolwich SE18
Greenwich Architect's Department
Borough architect: John M. Moore
1973–5

New Place Square, Four Squares Estates, Bermondsey SE16
Southwark Department of Architecture and Planning
Borough architect and planner: F.O. Hayes
Designed from 1969, built in 1971–5

Chalmer's Walk, Brandon Estate, Kennington SE17
GLC Department of Architecture and Civic Design
1974–6

Milford Towers, Catford SE6
Owen Luder Partnership for Lewisham London Borough Council
1969–74

Grovehill Court, Hildenborough Gardens, Bromley BR1
Peter Moro & Partners for the GLC
1975–7

Right: Wells Park Road, Wells Park Estate, Sydenham SE26
Lewisham Architect's Department
Borough architect: Julian Tayler
1976

Falcon Point, Bankside SE1
Southwark Development Department
Director of development: Ceri Griffiths
Borough architect: H.P. Trenton
1976–7

Eynsford House, Congreve Estate, Walworth SE17
Peter Moro & Partners for Southwark London Borough Council
1975–7

Pomeroy Street, Peckham SE14
Peter Moro & Partners for Southwark London Borough Council
1974–8

Alscot Way, Setchell Estate, Bermondsey SE1
Neylan & Ungless for Southwark London Borough Council
Designed from 1971, built in 1976–8

Somerville Road Estate, New Cross SE20
Howell Killick Partridge & Amis for Lewisham London Borough Council
Partner in charge: John Partridge
Commissioned in 1973, built in 1975–8

St Domingo House, Woolwich Dockyard Estate, Woolwich SE18
Greenwich Architect's Department
Borough architect: John M. Moore. Project architect: Elsie Sargent
Consulting engineers: Norman & Dawbarn
Planned from 1972, designed in 1973–4, built in 1974–80

Millender Walk, Silverlock Estate, Rotherhithe SE16
Stock, Page & Stock in association with the Southwark Development Department
Director of development: Ceri Griffiths
Borough architect: H.P. Trenton
1971–8

17a and 17b Longton Avenue, Sydenham SE26
Walter Segal's Lewisham self-build group in association with the
Lewisham Architect's Department
Borough architect: Julian Tayler

Deputy borough architect: Brian Richardson
First phase (Segal Close, Ormanton Road, Elstree Hill,
Longton Avenue)
1977–80

SOUTH-WEST

1. Lambeth

2. Wandsworth

3. Richmond upon Thames

4. Kingston upon Thames

5. Merton

6. Croydon

7. Sutton

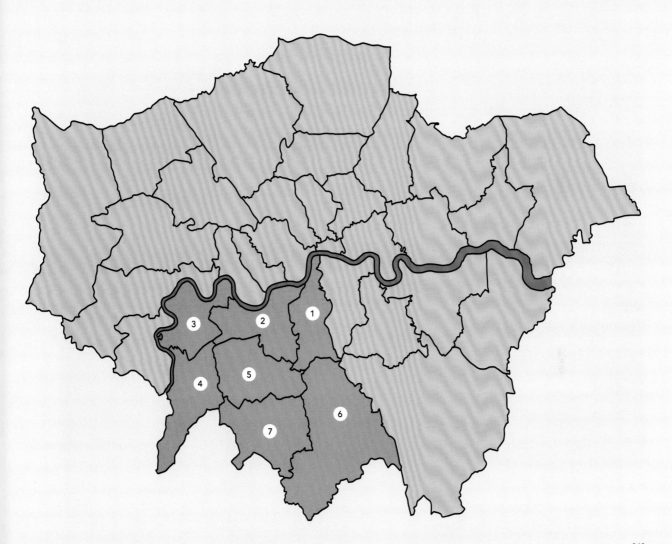

Fernwood, Wimbledon Park Estate, Southfields SW19
Wandsworth Architect's Department
Borough architect: W.H. Beesley
1947–53

Gipsy Road Gardens 'prefabricated permanent houses', West Norwood SE27
Wates for Lambeth Borough Council
Project architect at Wates: Kenneth W. Bland
1945–8

Cambridge Gardens Estate, Norbiton KT1
S. Clough Son & Partners for Kingston-upon-Thames Corporation
1947–9

Busby House, Streatham Park Estate, Aldrington Road, Tooting SW16
LCC Architect's Department
1951

Goodbehere House, Benton's Lane Estate, West Norwood SE27
Booth & Ledeboer for Lambeth Borough Council
1952–5

Beaumont House, Laburnum Road Estate, Mitcham CR2
Collcut & Hamp for Mitcham Borough Council
1953

Shelburne House, Fayland Estate, Mithcam Lane, Tooting SW16
LCC Architect's Department
1952–4

Right: Oatlands Court, Wimbledon Park Side SW19
LCC Architect's Department
Architect in charge: Colin Lucas
Project architects: H.H. Gillett and A.P. Roach
Designed from 1948, built in 1952–3

Eastwick Court and Wainford Close, Ackroydon East Estate SW19
LCC Architect's Department
Architect in charge: H.G. Gillett. Project architect: A.P. Roach
Designed in 1950, built in 1952–3

Community Centre, Ackroydon East Estate, Monfort Place SW19
LCC Architect's Department
Designed in 1950, built in 1952–3

Hindhead Point, Alton East Estate, Roehampton SW15
LCC Architect's Department
Architect in charge: Rosemary Stjernstedt
Project architects: Oliver Cox, A.W. Cleeve Barr, Michael Powell, J.N. Wall and H.P. Harrison
Designed in 1951, built in 1952–5, Grade II listed

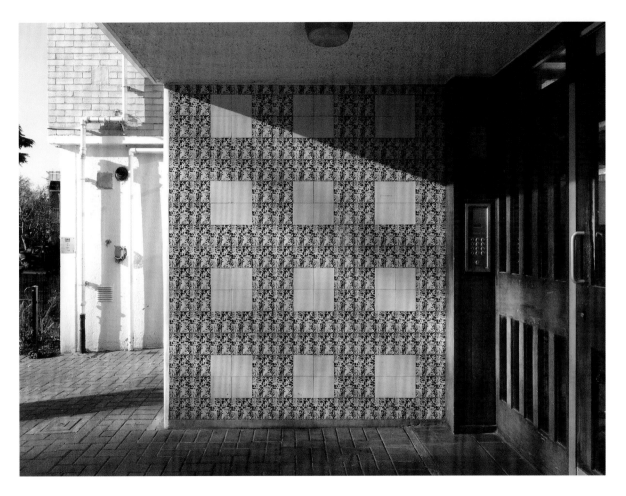

Hindhead Point, Alton East Estate, Roehampton SW15
LCC Architect's Department
Architect in charge: Rosemary Stjernstedt
Decorative tiles by Oliver Cox
Designed in 1951, built in 1952–5, Grade II listed

Woodhall House, Fitzhugh Estate, Trinity Road, Wandsworth SW18
LCC Architect's Department
Architects in charge: Rosemary Stjernstedt, Oliver Cox and Kenneth Grieb. Decorative tiles by Oliver Cox
1953–6

Woodhall House, Fitzhugh Estate, Trinity Road, Wandsworth SW18
LCC Architect's Department
1953–5

Top: Dunbridge House, Denmead House, Charcot House, Winchfield House and Binley House, Alton West Estate, Roehampton SW15
LCC Architect's Department
Architect in charge: Colin Lucas
Project architects: John Partridge, Bill Howell, John Killick, Stan Amis, Kevin Campbell, J.R. Galley and Roy Stout
Designed in 1952–3, built in 1955–8
Grade II* listed

Bottom: 57–79 Ibsley Gardens, Ibsley, Alton West Estate, Roehampton SW15
LCC Architect's Department
Designed from 1955, built in 1957–8

Right: Winchfield House, Alton West Estate, Roehampton SW15
LCC Architect's Department
Designed in 1952–3, built in 1955–8
Grade II* listed

Portland House and McCormick House, St Martin's Estate, Tulse Hill SW2
Charles Lovett Gill & Partners for the LCC
1954–5

Stroudley House, Patmore Estate, Wandsworth SW8
De Metz & Birks for the LCC
Designed from 1950, built in 1951–5

Lusher House, Kersfield Estate, Putney SW15
LCC Architect's Department
1956

Leda Court, Caldwell Gardens Estate, Oval SW9
Bridgwater & Shepheard for Lambeth Borough Council
1957

Woodchurch House, Cowley Estate, Brixton Road SW9
LCC Architect's Department
1955–7

Winterfold Close, Albert Drive, Wandsworth SW19
LCC Architect's Department
Designed from 1952, built in 1957–61

Allbrook House and Roehampton Library, Alton West Estate SW15
LCC Architect's Department
Project architects: John Partridge and Roy Stout
1957–61

Kettleby House, Loughborough Estate, Loughborough Junction, Lambeth SW9
LCC Architect's Department
Project architects: Colin Lucas, C.G. Weald, H.J. Hall, G.M. Sarson, E.J. Voisey, S.J. Howard,
A.A. Baker, Colin St John Wilson, Peter Carter and Alan Colquhoun
Planned and designed from 1952, built in 1956–8

Crownstone Road 35–107 and 1–33, St Matthew's Estate, Brixton SW2
LCC Architect's Department
1955–8

Dumain Court, Cottington Close Estate, Kennington SE11
Co-operative Planning Ltd for Lambeth Borough Council
1954–8

Whittaker Court, Studley Estate, Stockwell SW4
Sir Lancelot Keay, Basil G. Duckett & Partners for Lambeth Borough Council
1953–9

10–24 Lebanon Road, Longstaff Estate, Wandsworth SW18
LCC Architect's Department
1962

Whitlock Drive, Edgecombe Hall Estate, Southfields SW19
Clifford Culpin & Partners for Wandsworth Borough Council
1961–3

39–65 Askill Drive, Portinscale Estate West, East Putney SW15
Richard S. Nickson for Wandsworth Borough Council
Designed from 1960, built in 1962

Weisman House, Gipsy Hill SE19
Lambeth Architect's Department
Borough architect: Edward Hollamby
Designed from 1963, built in 1965

Right: Amesbury Tower, Durrington Tower and Fovant Court, Westbury
Estate, Wandsworth Road SW8
LCC Architect's Department
Architect in charge: Colin Lucas
Project architect: Philip Bottomley
Designed from 1961, completed by the GLC Department of Architecture
and Civic Design in 1968

Balaam House, Collingwood Grounds, Sutton
Sutton and Cheam Engineer's Department
Borough engineer: C. Needham
Chief architect: P.H. Masters
1964–5

Denmark Road, South Norwood, Croydon SE25
Croydon Engineer and Surveyor's Department
Borough engineer and surveyor: A.F. Holt
1958

Fieldway Estate, New Addington, Croydon CR0
Riches & Blythin in association with the Croydon Engineer and Surveyor's Department
Borough engineer and surveyor: A.F. Holt
Designed from 1964, built and completed for Croydon London Borough Council in 1967

Top: John Parker Square and Sporle Court, Winstanley Estate,
Battersea SW11
George, Trew & Dunn for Battersea Borough Council
Planned from 1959, built in 1964–6

Bottom: 9–12 Thomas Baines Road, Winstanley Estate
Abstract patterning by William Mitchell & Associates

Right: Holland Rise House, Holland Rise and Whitebeam Close,
Clapham Road SW9
Lambeth Architect's Department
Borough architect: Edward Hollamby
Project architect: George Finch
1966–7

Fairford House, Ebenezer House and Hurley House, Cottons Gardens Estate, Kennington Lane SE11
Lambeth Architect's Department
Borough architect: Edward Hollamby. Project architect: George Finch
1966–7

Edrich House, Studley Estate, Binfield Road SW4
Lambeth Architect's Department
Borough architect: Edward Hollamby. Project architect: George Finch
1968

Top: 46–97 Dovet Court, Mursell Estate, Clapham Road, Stockwell SW8
LCC Architect's Department
Project architect: William Jacoby
Designed from 1961, built in 1963–6

Bottom: The undercroft of 1–45 Dovet Court, Mursell Estate

Right: Lambeth Towers, Kennington Road SE11
Lambeth Architect's Department
Borough architect: Edward Hollamby
Project architect: George Finch
Assistant architects: R. Redsull and D. Gale
Designed in 1964–5, completed in 1971

Lennox Estate, Upper Richmond Road, Roehampton SW15
Gollins Melvin Ward & Partners for the GLC
Designed from 1965, built in 1968–72

Cambridge Road Estate, Norbiton KT1
Kingston Architect's Department
Borough architect: J.H. Lomas
1967–72

Central Hill Estate (and shop), Central Hill, Crystal Palace Hill SE19
Lambeth Directorate of Development Services
Director of development: Edward Hollamby
Project architect: Rosemary Stjernstedt
Assistant architects: Brian Roberts, Frank de Marco and
Adrian Sansom
Presented in 1966, built in 1967–74 (Phase I) and 1972–5 (Phase II)

Left: Teversham Lane and Kelvedon House, Spurgeon Estate,
Stockwell SW8
LCC Architect's Department
Designed from 1963, built by the GLC Department of Architecture
and Civic Design in 1966–7

Copeland House, Garratt Lane, Tooting SW17
R. Seifert & Partners for Wandsworth London Borough Council
Designed from 1967, built in 1971–2

Right: Hayesend House and Hazelhurst Road 2–10 (even),
Hazelhurst Estate, Tooting SW17
R. Seifert & Partners for Wandsworth London Borough Council
1968–72

Surrey Lane Estate, Battersea SW11
R. Seifert & Partners for Wandsworth London Borough Council
1969–71

Eastfields, Acacia Road, Mitcham CR4
Merton Architect's Department
Borough architect: Bernard V. Ward
1974

Ducavel House, Palace Road Estate, Tulse Hill SW2
GLC Department of Architecture and Civic Design
Project architects: Martin Douglas and Barbara Nash
1973

Top: Sadler Close Estate, Mitcham CR4
Merton Architect's Department
Borough architect: Bernard V. Ward
1972

Bottom: Longford Walk, Cressingham Gardens, Tulse Hill SW2
Lambeth Directorate of Development Services
Director of development: Edward Hollamby
1971–7

Opposite
Top left: Dyers Lane Estate, Upper Richmond Road, Putney SW15
Richmond Technical Services Department
Project architects: James Wood and Carlos Pyres
Chief architect: M.J.C. Edwards
1979

Top right: Britannia Close, Bowlands Road Estate, Clapham SW4
Darbourne & Darke for Lambeth London Borough Council
Designed from 1974, built in 1978–86

Bottom left: Church Green, Myatts Field South, Brixton SW9
Lambeth Directorate of Development Services
Director of development: Edward Hollamby
1971–8

Bottom right: Hazelwood, Benhill Grounds, Brunswick Road, Sutton SM1
Sutton Department of Technical Services
Borough architect: Peter J. Hirst
1978–9

Top: Friar Mews, Hainthorpe Estate, West Norwood SE27
Lambeth Directorate of Development Services
Director of development: Edward Hollamby
Presented in 1975, built in 1977–82

Bottom: 67–75 Dunbar Street, Dunbar & Dunelm Estate,
West Norwood SE27
Lambeth Directorate of Development Services
Director of development: Edward Hollamby
Project architect: Magda Borowiecka
Presented in 1974, built in 1977–80

Right: Southwyck House, Coldharbour Lane, Brixton SW9
Lambeth Directorate of Development Services
Director of development: Edward Hollamby
Project architect: Magda Borowiecka
Designed from 1969, built in 1973–81

INDEX OF ESTATES

Acknowledgements

London Estates has been adapted from the posts on my Instagram account, @notreallyobsessive. I am very grateful to its followers and commenters for their support and enthusiasm, as well as reminiscences about council housing in the capital. Those posts also led to my first exhibitions and to this book. Damon and Stephen at FUEL: truly, I couldn't wish for better publishers.

For all their help in my research I would like to thank the staff in the library of the Royal Institute of British Architects; the London Metropolitan Archives; the local history centres and archives in Barking and Dagenham, Bexley, Brent, Camden, the City of Westminster, Croydon, Enfield, Hackney, Haringey, Royal Borough of Kensington and Chelsea, Lambeth, Newham, Islington, Southwark, Sutton, Tower Hamlets and Wandsworth; and Wates Group.

For additional research I am indebted to the University of Edinburgh's *The Tower Block UK* project, *Survey of London*, the Twentieth Century Society and Historic England.

It was my father, Jože Zupančič, who was the first to tell me about the role and purpose of council housing, starting in Slovenia and Austria; and so many other things besides.

The book would be very different without the friendship and encouragment of the following people: Catherine Croft, Rut Blees Luxemburg, Brenna Horrox, Uta Kögelsberger, Chris McCormack, Terry McCormack, John Boughton, Owen Hatherley, Barnabas Calder, Wolfgang Tillmans, Philip Marshall, Eustace, John Grindrod, James Bainbridge, Alex Linsdell, Daniel Hopwood, Stephen Jay-Taylor, Steve Hodgson, Michael Heyward, Gunnar Klack, R.J. Wolfgang-Larsen, Richard Brook, Lukas Novotny, Mandy Payne, Irena Predalič, Miloš Kosec, Peter Žargi, Bogo Zupančič, Michael Rowley, James Lister, Marko Brožič, Edo Džafić, Alexander Roessner and Aki Takigawa. My thanks to them all. TZ

Published in 2024

FUEL Design & Publishing
33 Fournier Street
London E1 6QE

fuel-design.com
@fuelpublishing

Designed and edited by Murray & Sorrell FUEL
Photographs and text © Thaddeus Zupančič

Distribution by Thames & Hudson / D. A. P.
ISBN: 978-1-7398878-4-1
Printed in China

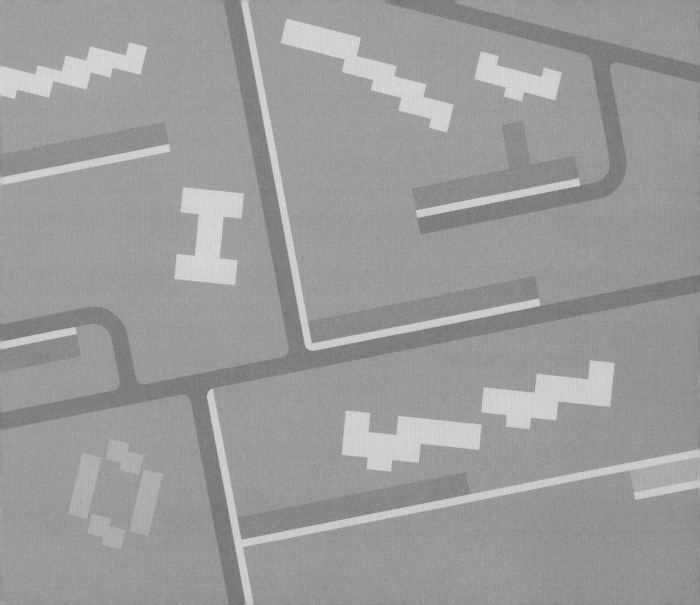